D1033134

Campaigns in Palestine
from Alexander the Great

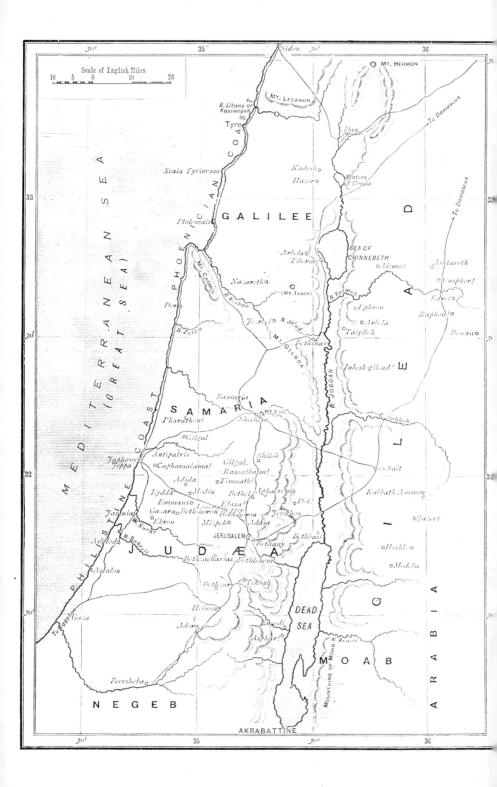

THE BRITISH ACADEMY

Campaigns in Palestine from Alexander the Great

By

Israel Abrahams

M.A. (Camb. and Lond.)

Reader in Talmudic and Rabbinic Literature in the University of
Cambridge ; Hon. Lit.D., Western Pennsylvania ; Hon. D.D.,
Hebrew Union College, Cincinnati

ARGONAUT, INC., PUBLISHERS
CHICAGO   MCMLXVII

Library of Congress Catalogue Card No. 67-31061

Unchanged reprint of the Schweich Lectures of 1922
Published by the British Academy in 1927.

PREFACE

THESE three lectures on 'Campaigns in Palestine from Alexander the Great' were delivered by the late Dr. Israel Abrahams before the British Academy in London, on December 14, 18, and 19, 1922. He continued to work at them, so far as other engagements and increasing ill-health permitted, but was not spared to give them the finishing touches. At his lamented death on October 6, 1925, the manuscript was practically ready for printing, and little remained to be done when I was requested to see it through the press. From conversations with him I had gathered that he contemplated a map, and a map has accordingly been provided, for which acknowledgements are due to the Cambridge University Press. Further, he intended to reproduce at least one coin, and it is hoped that what has been done in this respect would have met his wishes. Thanks are due to Dr. G. F. Hill, of the British Academy, Keeper of Coins and Medals, British Museum, for his courtesy in providing casts of the coins on the Plate. It is known too that, had he lived, Dr. Abrahams would have made some expansions and added appendices, e. g. on Bar Cochba's revolt (p. 38). I believe also, from a certain conversation, that he would have had something to say on evidence for the way in which the Romans in the course of billeting soldiers upon the Jews had helped to provoke the Jewish Revolt; and I conceive that the query on p. 31 (middle), concerning the elephants who were *shown* the blood of grapes, implies that he might have had more

to say on that subject.[1]   Apart from the correction of a few
slight inconsistencies and two or three minor adjustments
the Lectures appear in the form in which the author left
them.   The Index has been prepared by Mr. Herbert Loewe
M.A., University Lecturer in Rabbinic Hebrew, Oxford,
from whose hands a memoir of this great Jewish scholar
may shortly be expected.

The subject-matter which Dr. Abrahams selected for the
Schweich Lectures was one on which he had something
new to contribute.   His knowledge of the topography and
history of Palestine enabled him to treat it as few others
could have done, and these pages will be found to contain
much that is suggestive to those who are more particularly
interested in the military aspects.   Apart from Sir George
Adam Smith's great classic, *The Historical Geography of the
Promised Land*, and a couple of special monographs on the
battles fought by the Egyptians at Megiddo (1479 B.C.) and
Kadesh (1288 B.C.),[2] the military history of Palestine does
not seem to have attracted the attention of experts that it
deserves.   But the Old Testament narrative itself, and the
Amarna Letters with their records of guerilla wars and of
more extensive campaigning in Palestine and Syria, together
with miscellaneous data from the Graeco-Roman period,
afford no little store of material had Dr. Abrahams desired
to go back and start before the days of Alexander the Great

---

[1] 1 Macc. vi. 34.   Dr. Oesterley (Charles's *Apocrypha and Pseudepigrapha*,
vol. i, p. 88) refers to the practice of exciting elephants by giving them liquor
to drink (*cf.* Aelian, *De Animal.* xiii. 8); and the story in 3 Macc. v, tells how
elephants could thus be maddened and let loose upon Jews confined in the
hippodrome of Alexandria.   We might suppose that 'shown' is an easy mis-
understanding of 'intoxicated' (*hir'u* for *hirwu* in the Hebrew); although it
could be urged (with Dr. Oesterley) that in the passage under discussion 'the
liquor was only shown to them, for had they drunk of it they would have got
out of control'.   (Mr. Loewe also refers me to 'must' in *Hobson-Jobson*, p. 604
[Yule and Burnell, ed. Crooke, 1903].)
[2] H. H. Nelson, *The Battle of Megiddo*, (Beirut, 1913); J. H. Breasted, *The
Battle of Kadesh : A Study in the earliest known Military Strategy* (Chicago, 1903);
see also the *Cambridge Ancient History*, vol. ii, pp. 69 and 143 sqq.

and amplify his treatment. On the other hand, it is precisely the Maccabean age and the Jew's fight for freedom which to him were of the first importance, and it was natural for him to pass from that fight to General Allenby's deliverance of Jerusalem from the Turk, and treat these and intervening campaigns from a 'comparative' point of view.

To the study of the Maccabees Dr. Abrahams had devoted himself in the past; and readers will notice with what precision he is thereby able to handle some of the more difficult questions of criticism which the Books of the Maccabees bring.[1] The actual Maccabean campaigns themselves, in all their details, have recently been studied with admirable fullness by the eminent Dominican scholar Father Abel;[2] but their significance has never perhaps been handled with such enthusiasm and insight, nor the 'comparative' method so instructively employed as in these pages.

That the campaigns in Palestine deserve a much higher position among the decisive battles of the world (p. 2) is a view which is intelligible and excusable, the more so as military events which shaped or reshaped the history of the 'least of all lands' naturally make a special appeal to biblical students. Nor can one deny that the triumph of Judaism through the victories of the Maccabees was part of the great Oriental reaction against Hellenism, and that it preserved the Old Testament and thus formed the prelude to Christianity. It must, of course, be granted that such a technical question as that of the true part played by sea-power (p. 43) should have been discussed on the basis of a larger body

---

[1] See, for example, his remarks upon Willrich (p. 12 sq.).
[2] See the *Revue Biblique*, 1923, pp. 495–521; 1924, pp. 201–17; 1925, pp. 194–216; 1926, pp. 206–22 (incomplete), with plans and illustrations.

of facts, and with attention both to the use made by
Egypt of the Phoenician ports and to the perennial rivalry
of Palestine (with Egypt) and Syria (with Asia Minor, &c.).
And other criticisms from the point of view of military
science could be brought. But these are slight compared
with the breadth of view with which Dr. Abrahams has
succeeded in treating his subject ; he opens up a wide field,
and many classes of reader will find his observations highly
suggestive.[1]

It is this breadth and versatility which made him so
invaluable a guide. His judgements were scrupulously just—
one never heard even an unkind utterance from his lips.
He was keenly discriminating in his arguments—witness
his attitude to Antiochus Epiphanes (p. 17), and he was
the last man to strive to make a point unfairly. How wide
his interests were is seen, for example, in his note on the
Poetry of Space (p. 18 n). He was singularly well-read,
a good speaker, and a master of style. His writings were
polished, and—witness his well-known *Studies in Pharisaism*
—the fruit of careful and scholarly labour. He was of the
generation of Driver, Cheyne, and others, and took part
with these in popularizing a liberal attitude to the Old
Testament. More than that, as was said of him in the
well-merited obituary notice in *The Times* of October 7, 1925,
he interpreted Judaism to the Christians and Christianity
to the Jews. One gained more from him in talk and
counter-talk even than from his writings, and indeed there
were those who found that they could talk more intimately
to this son of Israel than to their co-religionists.

[1] Brigadier-General Costello, D.S.O., to whom I am indebted for some
valuable remarks, points out to me, apropos of an invader from the *south*
entering Jerusalem from the *north* (see p. 11 sq.), that the meeting-place of
General Allenby and the Mayor of Jerusalem was north-west of the city, and
on the Jaffa road.

Special honour was paid to his memory by the University of Cambridge in the Memorial Service in the Senate House on October 22, 1925. It was a tribute to his learning and to his influence on behalf of scholarship and mutual understanding. In Schiller-Szinessy, Schechter, and Abrahams Talmudic studies reached a high level in this University, and the last two, and above all Israel Abrahams, established a tradition for liberal scholarship which, it is sincerely to be hoped, friends of Judaism will never allow to expire. May this posthumous publication of his last lectures call attention to the gap and the necessity of filling it!

How helpful he was and how authoritative his learning may best be said in the words of Professor Burkitt, F.B.A.:

'Of all the Jewish scholars I have known Israel Abrahams was the most helpful to the student of Christian origins. It was not merely that he was a good Talmudist and had a good acquaintance with Philo as well: in addition to this he had a real understanding of what modern critical study aims at. He was an acceptable preacher and a pastor to Jewish undergraduates and B.A.'s, while at the same time he thoroughly understood the charm that the historical investigator of the Past finds in the search for objective truth, apart from its ethical appeal or controversial value— a very rare cast of mind! His wide reading and his technical learning combined to give him a sure instinct for what in the pagan and Christian literature of the century before and after the current Era was, or was not, compatible with a Jewish origin: it was this knowledge and instinct combined that made him an invaluable colleague, and it is for this especially, besides his noble personal qualities, that makes his loss so perceptible.'

My own acquaintance with Israel Abrahams goes back

a quarter of a century, when he was a contributor to the
Encyclopaedia Biblica; and I would hope that the small
labour in seeing these Lectures through the press will be
a slight return for much courtesy and encouragement which
I received from him from the very first. If I close with
words well known to every Jew, it is because the work of
this ' scholar ' was for the ' increase of peace ', not for Israel
alone, but ' for the world '; and, true to Rabbi Eleazar's
famous saying, his labours for co-operation and harmony
knew no limits of creed or class.

תלמידי חכמים מרבים שלום בעולם

STANLEY COOK.

CONTENTS

CAMPAIGNS IN PALESTINE

LECTURE I

THE Schweich Trust allows a wide choice of subjects; for, though Archaeology properly stands first in the list, History also appears in it. It would be a mistake, indeed, to treat Archaeology, even in its narrower sense, as limited to the work of the excavator's spade, or to the discovery of concrete relics of the past. Such objects merely arouse curiosity, or, as in the new Thebes finds, excite attention as treasure-trove, until their place in the history of the human spirit is determined. Archaeology is, in fact, a branch of the science of history.

Hence, though in the present course much reliance is ultimately placed on topographical research, yet its main purpose is less to present facts than to explain them; less the actual description of campaigns than the unravelling of their deeper causes and more lasting effects in history remote and recent. The circumstance that the lecturer has no expert military competence may, it is hoped, be less detrimental than must at first sight appear inevitable. Yet the lecturer is fully conscious of his limitations even within the lines indicated.

Let me begin with Sir Edward Creasy, whose book, *The Fifteen Decisive Battles of the World*, was at one time very widely read. It has possibly acquired a new lease of popularity, for it has recently been included in the 'Oxford Editions of Standard Authors'. Surveying the recorded scenes of carnage from Marathon to Waterloo, Creasy does not include a single conflict on Palestinian soil. In one sense this is a just exclusion. Just as Palestine is a unique land, so its battles have been unique. Until Allenby's great hour the campaigns in Palestine had been somewhat, though not entirely, unimportant from the military point of view. True, no area of the earth's surface has so often re-echoed to the tramp of armed men as the short strip which

B

stretches from Tyre to Gaza. Even the migrations of races were of the nature of campaigns; the ancient world knew no peaceful penetrations, but rushes red in tooth and claw. For more than four thousand years the story is continuous of armies and caravans moving by this road to battle and to trade. The secular antagonisms of North and South, the great rivalries of the Near East, found here battle-grounds or routes to battle-grounds. If ever soil should have been indelibly incarnadined, it was the sand-dunes of the Palestinian shore, and the low hills bordering the Shephelah. Yet, though we find here the clearest signs of the ruinous effects of wars in the destruction of ancient cities, we find the barest military traces, and even excavations have brought to light few of the relics of struggle such as the Flanders fields are constantly revealing. And if sparsely inhabited mounds now replace once densely populated sites, thriving agricultural colonies nowadays mark the track so often devastated by warring hordes: the new land itself is triumphing over its olden ravagers and despoilers.

If, then, Creasy's verdict as to decisiveness of battles were decisive criticism, we would seem, in this course of lectures, to be engaged on an insignificant survey. But modern inquiry has altogether changed our estimate of values, and Creasy himself relieves our premonitions of futility by citing a remark of Hallam's in definition of 'decisive' as applied to wars. Decisive battles are those of which it may be said that 'a contrary event would have essentially varied the drama of the world in all its subsequent stages'. Applying this test, and even if we limit our attention to the second half only of the recorded campaigns in Palestine, to the period stretching between Alexander and Allenby, it is clear that the campaigns in Palestine are actually among the most decisive of history. Had Alexander the Great failed to take Tyre, had the Seleucids overwhelmed the Maccabees in the Beth-horon passes, had Jerusalem successfully resisted Titus' onslaught from Scopus, had Julius Severus met his match in Bar-Cochba, had Richard the First penetrated to the Holy City, had Napoleon not been foiled at Acre, had Napier's guns abstained from bombarding the Palestinian coast in the interests of Turkey and to the detriment of Mohammed Ali, or had Allenby been deterred by the theorists of the Western Front from his glorious sweep from Cairo to Damascus—any of these events, contrary to the actual event, must have materially altered the whole aspect of history.

Admittedly, along this line of reasoning lies the open road of exaggeration. Gibbon shows us an example when he attributes to Charles Martel's victory over the Saracens at Tours the delivery of Christian civilization from the domination of Islam. ' But for Charles the Hammer ', says Gibbon, ' perhaps the interpretation of the Koran would be taught in the schools of Oxford, and her pulpits might demonstrate to a circumcised people the sanctity and truth of the revelation of Mahomet '. Similarly it is too much to claim, with Hatch, for that earlier Hammer, Judas the Maccabee, that but for his victories the world would have lost the inspiration of Hebraism, so that while Christendom might still have possessed the Nicene Creed it would never have had the Sermon on the Mount. Nevertheless, when we consider the lasting influence of the Maccabean campaigns on the relations between Hellenism and Hebraism, we may doubt the judgement which impels Creasy to admit as decisive the victory of General Gates at Saratoga over Burgoyne in the American War of Independence in 1777, and to omit Judas' triumph over Nicanor at Adasa in the Judean War of Independence some 2,000 years sooner. The effects of Judas' success were still influential when mother England retired from the contest with her daughter Colony across the Atlantic. The science of Theology is often decried by historians, but it has been the theologians and not the historians who have understood in this matter.

The incidents of our own time prove that battles are not to be priced by their immediate results. We have witnessed the apparent finality of Sedan undone on the Marne. Napoleon's seemingly decisive victory at Jena was even shorter-lived than von Moltke's. History teaches us to distrust the decisiveness of human decisions. On the morrow of the Moorish conquest of Spain in the eighth century, the Christian reconquest began. On the other hand, Creasy excluded from his list of decisive battles the Crusades, conceiving no doubt that as they left Palestine in Mohammedan hands as they found it before the Crusade began, they therefore had left no impress on human affairs. In point of fact they left a great impress, illustrating, as no other Palestinian campaigns have done, the romantic action and reaction of East on West. The Maccabean campaigns show us the spiritual action and reaction of the same Oriental and Occidental forces. The Maccabees have an interest for the history of culture, the Crusades for the story of chivalry.

To deal fully with our subject, it would seem imperative to survey the history of the near East for several thousands of years. This is impossible, and fortunately it is not necessary. It would be fascinating to picture the scenes enacted on Palestinian soil in the first recorded invasion of it by Egypt when, three-and-a-half millennia before the Christian era, Pepi's troop-ships carried an army to make reprisals on the Beduin raiders, 'Sand-dwellers of the Land of the Gazelle Nose'. Seemingly the Palestinian highlands as well as the coast were penetrated. ' I came and smote them all, and every revolter among them was slain '—so boasts Pepi's general. This occurred *circa* 2800 B.C.; and the record is of interest because we observe thus early the influence of sea-power. Command of the sea has never sufficed of itself to hold Palestine—this was proved in the Crusades. On the other hand, without command of the sea, land-successes were equally futile, as was proved by the fate of Napoleon at Acre. The older Pharaohs combined sea- with land-power. They garrisoned and provisioned the coast-cities, and, besides storing them with spare masts and spars for naval repairs, used them as bases for land-marches. What we know of their methods throws light on subsequent campaigns of which we really know less. The Pharaohs exacted supplies from the neighbouring tribes, fortified the wells and defended the cisterns on the desert route from Egypt into Palestine. Otherwise the desert would have been an impassable barrier. The water-supply has been a recurrent trouble ; Allenby also experienced it. We know, again, that the armies involved in these early campaigns were small ; rarely exceeding 20,000 men. Similarly, Alexander the Great started out to conquer Egypt with but 10,000 more, and Napoleon commanded about as many in his Syrian campaign. But we must pass over all these early Egyptian campaigns, noting, however, that Thotmes III once captured Jaffa—the scene of the Perseus-Andromeda myth—' by introducing picked soldiers into the town, concealed in panniers, borne by a train of donkeys '. Breasted sees in this tale a probable prototype of the story of Ali Baba and the Forty Thieves. It also reminds us of the stratagem of the Wooden Horse at Troy.

But we must pass all this over, nor may we stay to consider the wars between Egypt and northern dynasts for control of Palestine and Syria; we must deny ourselves the spirited narrative of the youthful Rameses II winning, as the Court poet puts it, a single-handed victory over the Hittites at Kadesh ; we cannot witness the appearance of the Assyrians, nor discuss the pitiful struggles of Israel and Judah against each other and against the Philistines, nor rest on the northern invasions which inspired eighth-century prophets, the mighty Scythian raids which forced Jeremiah to speak, the campaigns of Sennacherib, Sargon, and Nebuchadnezzar, or the coming of Persia which gave substance to the noble dreams of Deutero-Isaiah. What a marvellous tale all this would be, from Merneptah's vain boast that he had made a final end of Israel, to the Return from the Babylonian Exile. It is because of the need to confine ourselves to reasonable limits, and because the effects of all these earlier events are so clearly seen after Alexander, that we make him our starting-point.

For, whatever be our verdict on Alexander's actual achievements, his name is rightly associated with a vital change in the aspect of the world. Asiatic Hellenism preceded his campaigns, and its full organization succeeded his death. Yet it is futile to deny to him the epithet great. Mr. Wells protests that Alexander ' created no tradition, nothing more than a personal legend '.

How could he create a tradition, when he died at an age when most men have not yet begun to find themselves? It was just his 'personal legend' that counted, and gave Ptolemies and Seleucids their inspiration and opportunity. I particularly mention these, because the Hellenization which most affected history concerned Egypt and Syria, with Palestine between. For this reason, the most significant of Alexander's victories was not won at Arbela but at Issus. Early in the spring of 334 B.C. Alexander left Macedonia with not much over 30,000 infantry and 5,000 cavalry, crossed the Hellespont, triumphed at the Granicus, cut the Gordian knot, won the battle of Issus, and then turned, not northwards into the interior of Asia Minor, but southwards towards the Palestinian coast-route to Egypt, where his stay in the winter of 332–331 was made memorable for all time by the foundation of Alexandria.

Insufficient note has been made by historians of a remarkable coincidence. In the earlier campaign which culminated in his peaceful occupation of Egypt, Alexander passed through several of the sites associated afterwards, in the reverse order, with the momentous journeys of Paul. The chief places familiar to us in the *Acts* and *Epistles*, Rome of course excepted, occur also in Arrian's *Anabasis of Alexander*—Sardis and Ephesus, Tarsus, Miletus, Halicarnassus, and the rest. Without pushing the parallel too closely, it may be said that Paul's spiritual campaigns were the return march of the martial campaigns of Alexander. The Macedonian was the forerunner of the Christian, Paul's missionary ancestor was Alexander. But much was necessary between. If the East was to reassert itself on the West, the East had first to organize itself in the heart of the Oriental Hellenization. The firm establishment of Hebraism as a force in the Hellenic world had to come before Christianity could enter into the legacy both of Greece and Judea without superseding either. It is a false epigram that Athens and Jerusalem died that the world might live by them. Neither Greece nor Judea died to give birth to western civilization—for both are immortal, each in and for itself, and it is on that immortality that western

civilization is reared. Regarded, anyhow, as the turning-point
in the relations of East to West, Alexander's campaign along the
Palestinian coast, his seven months' siege of Tyre and his two
months' siege of Gaza, must be placed first for importance among
the episodes of his amazing career, among the decisive moments
in all history.

And here a fascinating problem confronts us. Did Alexander
come into direct contact with the Jews during his Palestinian
campaign? Did he visit Jerusalem? The Greek historians are
silent on the matter, and from this silence it has been inferred
that the legend-coloured statements of Josephus and the Talmud
are altogether untrue. But the silence of the Greeks is no
criterion. Herodotus, curious as he was about cults, had no
curiosity about Judaism. Polybius certainly intended to write
an account of Jerusalem, but he either abandoned the intention,
or the chapters in which he fulfilled it have been lost. But the
most significant instance is Plutarch. His whole concern with
the Jews was what he called their idleness on the Sabbath, while
he seriously raised the question whether they worshipped
Dionysus, and whether they abstained from swine's flesh because
they venerated or loathed the creature. In his life of Pompey,
Plutarch entirely omits the perfectly-authenticated Judean campaign of Caesar's rival. Plutarch says nothing of Pompey's
entry into Jerusalem, which produced among other consequences
the so-called Psalms of Solomon. It is thus quite improbable that
the Greek historians of Alexander would have thought it worth
their while to record an excursion to Jerusalem even if it
occurred.

A priori, such an excursion is probable enough. Alexander
had a genuine, if romantic, interest in foreign shrines. His
history is full of that interest, though on this occasion I must
omit most of the evidence, except in so far as it affects Palestine.
One of his motives for determining to enter Tyre and not merely
to accept its submission, was his desire to visit the temple of the
Phoenician Melkart or Baal. Immediately after he left Palestine,
and on his first arrival in Egypt, he offered sacrifice to Apis and

summoned from Greece the most famous artists to take part in a musical display. His orgies in Oriental costume are well known. All this repeats itself in Napoleon. Alexander's Greek soldiery were disgusted at their leader's buffoonery, just as Napoleon's troopers laughed with ribald humour at his Oriental masquerades. The invaders of Palestine were on the whole an arrogant group, and we can not only pardon but even approve the olden Hebrew prophet's scathing attack on the vainglory of some of the earlier megalomaniacs. A noble exception, in much later times, was Omar. When in A.D. 637 the Caliph's generals captured Jerusalem, Omar yielded to the pressure of friend and foe alike and travelled to accept the submission of the Holy City. 'The simplicity of his journey,' writes Gibbon, 'is more illustrious than the royal pageants of vanity and oppression. The conqueror of Persia and Syria was mounted on a red camel, which carried, besides his person, a bag of corn, a bag of dates, a wooden dish, and a leathern bottle of water. Wherever Omar halted, the company was invited to partake of his homely fare, and the repast was consecrated by the prayer and exhortation of the Commander of the Faithful.'

Alexander certainly was not gifted with the simplicity of this child of the desert, yet was not altogether the victim of luxurious display. He was, as Plutarch shows us, two men in one. In his dealings with Asiatics, he was arrogant enough, as one 'firmly convinced of his divine parentage'. But he was modest in his dealings with the Greeks. Painfully wounded by an arrow, he said: 'This, my friends, is blood that flows from my wound, and not the ichor that courses through the veins of gods.' Altogether, we discern in Alexander a genuine curiosity as to foreign ways, an appreciation of Eastern cults, which not even his contemporary, Aristotle, matched. *A priori*, then, it is probable that, while in Palestine, he would have been attracted to the Temple in Jerusalem. He must have heard much about it in Persia. Even Graetz, who is sceptical as to the historicity of Alexander's visit to Judea, admits that it is a 'psychological possibility', and nowadays psychological possibilities seem to be the only facts.

There is another *a priori* point in favour of Josephus.   There
is a legendary element in his story which, so far from discrediting
it, really confirms it.   Josephus relates that during the siege of
Tyre, Alexander wrote to the Jewish High Priest, Jaddus, or
Jaddua, asking for auxiliaries and supplies, and bidding him
transfer allegiance from Persia to Macedonia, 'for he would
never repent of so doing', a promise well kept in the sequel.
But Jaddus refused, on the ground of his oath of fealty to Darius.
Scorn has been poured on this plea, and indeed Judea had latterly
had good reason to hate the Persians.   During the century before
the coming of Alexander, the Persian satraps and their underlings
'plundered the land, while a succession of Persian generals on
their way to Egypt brought it near famine through the vast
supplies of food which they demanded'.   Even nearer to
Alexander's siege of Tyre, the Temple was defiled by the Persian
general Bagoses, and it has been held that Jews joined in the
revolt in 363, as they certainly did a few years later.   Large
numbers of Jews were enslaved, some being deported as far as
Hyrcania by the Caspian Sea.   This was only a generation before
Alexander, so that the statement that Alexander was refused help
from Judea because of that country's allegiance to the Persian
king Darius seems unhistorical.   But we must remember that
revulsions of feeling with regard to despotic rulers were frequent
and sudden.   There is no record of unkindness to Judea on the
part of Darius.   In the course of the intrigues between the
Samaritans and Darius, it is quite possible that the High Priest
had given Darius a pledge of fealty, in order to counter a similar
offer from the other side.   We have an exact parallel in the third
Crusade.   Saladin was approached by Richard and Conrad with
rival proposals for peace.   The same thing may well have
happened in the case of Darius.

Be that as it may, Josephus records that Alexander, incensed
at the refusal of Judean aid, angrily threatened to secure his
demands by force, waiting only till he had stormed Tyre and
occupied Gaza.   Immediately after the latter exploit, Alexander
made haste to go up to Jerusalem.   Jaddus, at first alarmed, was

reassured by a dream, wherein he was admonished to march out, himself arrayed in purple and gold, mitred, and bearing on his forehead the gold plate on which was inscribed the Divine Name. With him he was to take the priests in sacerdotal attire of fine linen, and a mass of laymen, to greet Alexander as a friend. Alexander was accompanied by a large following of Phoenicians and Chaldeans, bent on plunder. To the astonishment of them all, and Parmenio in particular, Alexander adored the Name and saluted its bearer. 'Why this adoration of the priest,' asked Parmenio. 'I adored not him,' replied Alexander, 'but the God who has honoured him with his office. For I saw this very person in a dream in these very robes, when I was at Dium in Macedonia, who, when I was considering with myself whether I might obtain the dominion of Asia, exhorted me to make no delay, but boldly to cross over, for he would conduct my army and give me dominion over the Persians.' Seeing the very person of his dream in the robes of his vision, he felt confident that his ambitions were to be fulfilled. He then went up to the Temple, and under the High Priest's direction offered sacrifice, and was shown Daniel's prophecies. Next day he assented to Jaddus' petition that 'they might follow the laws of their fathers', pay no tribute every seventh year, and that similar concessions should be made to Jews elsewhere. Alexander 'willingly promised to do what was asked. And when he said to the people, that if any of them would enlist in his army, on condition that they should continue in the laws of their fore-fathers, he was willing to take them with him, many enlisted in his service.'

This story is no doubt fantastic, and may (as Dr. Büchler has argued) contain composite elements, especially in its reference to the Samaritans. My own conviction is that the Samaritan trouble was recurrent; that it was as active in the fourth century as it was in the second. But I am now discussing the broader question. It seems to me that the fantastic details provide no adequate ground for refusing to accept Josephus' main statement as historical; just as the differences in detail between Josephus and the Talmud do not disprove the fact underlying both accounts. Precisely the 'visionary' setting in both cases supports it. For Alexander was above all a visionary. Plutarch tells us how, 'during the seventh month of the siege of Tyre, Alexander dreamed that Heracles greeted him in a friendly manner from the city walls and called upon him to enter.' Again, when planning the building of a city in Egypt, ' he dreamed that a man with long hair and venerable aspect appeared to him ', and advised the choice of Pharos as the site of his new foundation. And Arrian, who is on the whole a sober historian, constantly records Alexander's reliance on omens, while the conqueror's Greek troops readily accepted them as valid. Josephus is thus in line with an authentic tradition of Alexander's temperament, and the visionary setting of his appearance at Jerusalem is quite true to type.

But it has been strongly argued that the Greek historians leave no loophole for a digression to Jerusalem, that in fact the time-scheme of Alexander's movements along the Palestinian coast makes it physically impossible for any excursion into the Judean hill-country. This argument is based on what, I submit, is a complete misreading of Arrian and the rest of the authorities. I must again omit here a full discussion of the evidence. The argument assumes that directly Gaza fell, Alexander proceeded by a forced march of seven days to Pelusium. This rapid advance towards Egypt certainly seems to leave no room for a detour to Jerusalem. But Arrian tells us no such thing. When he moved his army from Gaza to Egypt, Alexander's march was rapid, but he did not leave Gaza immediately on its fall. On the contrary there was much to be done before he left the place, and there is nothing in Arrian or Curtius to imply that time failed for such an experience as Josephus describes.

Equally inadmissible is the contention—repeated *ad nauseam* by modern critics—that the falsity of Josephus is shown by his ignorantly placing the meeting between Alexander and Jaddus in the north of Jerusalem, while Alexander must have approached the city from the south. This is an entire misconception. Both

Titus and Richard I approached Jerusalem from the south, and yet reached it on the north. Particularly noteworthy is it that Richard arrived at Beit Nuba from Ascalon, just as Alexander arrived at Scopus from Gaza. There was certainly a southern route from Gaza through Beersheba and the Hebron road to Jerusalem, and this was on the old caravan road. But what was probably the *normal* route, with an invader both acquainted with the interior and in full command of the coast, was to advance up the familiar coast, and to turn in eastwards from the neighbourhood of Jaffa. Thus Josephus was probably right in making king and priest meet north of Jerusalem. And with all respect to our learned moderns, though Josephus perhaps knew little about scientific geography, and may have thought Gerizim higher than Ebal, yet he possibly knew as much as we do of the practicable routes of his native land. He would hardly have allowed his narrative to contain so obvious a topographical 'howler' as some detect. In fact it is no 'howler' at all.

The subsequent influence of Alexander's Palestinian campaign on the civilization of the East does not, it is true, depend upon a visit to Jerusalem. But I have invited your close attention to this detail, partly because we should like it to be true, and even more because we shall do well to avoid Willrich's frame of mind, which makes it quite enough for Josephus to make a statement for the statement to be false. Moreover, it is worth while protesting against the tendency to subject an ancient historian to meticulous examination, and to conclude that his main assertions are overthrown if some of the details can be proved inaccurate. Documents of the past should not be so treated, and when they are, facts have a way of exacting their revenge. Willrich, in his onslaught on Josephus' contrary assertion, would have it that, apart from isolated instances, there were no Jewish settlers in Egypt until Ptolemy VII in the middle of the second century after Alexander. Recent discoveries have disproved this contention. In 1902 there was found, within an easy walk of Alexandria, an inscription dedicating a synagogue at least as old as Ptolemy III. But beyond that, the Elephantine papyri reveal the presence of an organized Jewish community in the Fayyum even before Alexander. Evidence is, in fact, accumulating that Ptolemy I, Alexander's immediate successor in Egypt, did, as an unjustly-suspected fragment of Hecataeus records, firmly settle Jews in Northern Egypt. All this tends to suggest that the favour which Hellenistic rulers—both Egyptian and Syrian— showed to the Jews was a legacy from Alexander's similar policy, derived from the support that his clemency won from the Jewish contemporaries of his invasion of the Holy Land.

When, however, I spoke of favourable treatment by Hellenistic rulers, I was referring to the Diaspora rather than to Palestine itself. There was little peace in that country while Egypt and Syria were struggling for its possession. Nothing in the history of Palestine is more painful reading than these struggles. They were fruitless in themselves ; they were dictated by no generous policy, but by motives of personal ambition or imperial expansion. From the moment of Alexander's death, as Driver expresses it, Phoenicia and Palestine were in an ambiguous position, a debate-able borderland between powerful rivals. I am not tempted to tell the tale in its details, as unedifying as they are complicated. 'On the whole, however, except during some brief intervals, Palestine remained subject to Egypt, until Antiochus the Great defeated the forces of Ptolemy Epiphanes in 198 B. C. at Paneion ', under the foot of Hermon, and near the sources of the Jordan. After that date Palestine passed permanently into the power of Syria. On the whole the Egyptian suzerainty had not been resented, but there was a reason why the change to Syrian domination was welcomed. At all events, though Rome over-threw Antiochus the Great at Magnesia, and imposed a humilia-ting peace on the harbourer of Hannibal, it did not interfere with the Syrian lordship over Palestine, until Pompey in 63 B. C. practically reduced it to the condition of a Roman province.

During this long and senseless struggle between Syria and Egypt, the country suffered materially, whatever the varying fortunes of the rivals. The people lost, whichever army won. The Judeans, and the inhabitants of Palestine generally, were so harassed that to cite Josephus' figure for the last pre-Maccabean phase, the land was ' like a ship in a storm, tossed by the waves on both sides '. Whether Antiochus the Great triumphed or endured reverses mattered little. Yet when Antiochus defeated the Egyptians at Paneion, the Jews received him without opposition into Jerusalem, ' gave plentiful provision to all his army and to his elephants ', and—a deed fraught with future disaster—helped to expel the Egyptian garrison from the Jeru-salem citadel and to replace it by a Syrian force. This Syrian garrison of the citadel was long a thorn in the side of the Maccabees. The concessions of Antiochus III were real enough, and it is possible that but for the wild schemes of Antiochus IV Judea might have settled down to peaceful loyalty to Syria. The Judeans showed no antipathy to Hellenism as such. They were forced into an unnatural antagonism. Freudenthal seems right in his conclusion that Hellenism had made way among the orthodox Jews as well as among the unorthodox. There are distinct indications of Hellenic thought in so conservative a writer as the author of *Ecclesiasticus*. That there was no natural antagonism was demonstrated later. Philo found for his form of Hebraism inspiration as much in Greek as in Jewish thought. His system is a harmonization of the two. Nor did he stand alone. Much later, Maimonides was almost as much dependent on Aristotle as on Moses for his ethical and metaphysical theories. Medieval scholasticism as a whole is an illustration of the possi-bility of bringing the Hellenic and Hebraic streams to a confluence. Hence, I feel justified in declaring that it was Antiochus IV who was responsible for making the inspirations of Greece and Judea seemed opposed and antagonistic.

There is another point. While Judea reluctantly passed from Persian to Macedonian suzerainty in the fourth century, it seems to have been more easily inclined to pass from the Ptolemaic to the Seleucid overlordship in the second century. But the readiness of the Judeans to transfer their allegiance from Egypt must not be attributed to fickleness nor charged with ingratitude. The Egyptian king, Ptolemy Philopator, seems in fact to have anticipated the ill-starred designs of Antiochus IV, both by a defilement of the Temple and an attack on Judaism. He seems to have been quite un-Egyptian in his plan to make citizenship dependent on religious conformity, an oppressive polity from which the West itself has but recently emerged, if it has yet emerged. This is the sense in which I read the historical kernel of the so-called *Third Book of the Maccabees.* Underlying it is a little-known Palestinian campaign which was not unimportant. Thus the Jews were thrown into the arms of the Syrians. Judea in the end paid dearly for the change. Antiochus IV proved a worse master than Ptolemy Philopator.

We have thus briefly surveyed the Palestinian campaigns for the century and a half that separated Alexander's descent on the coast to Antiochus IV's ascent by the same route. The one marched to Egypt in triumph, the other returned thwarted in the moment of victory. Inside the circle marked out on the Delta sand by the Roman legate, and forced to decide while he stood thus circumscribed, Antiochus yielded to Rome, but with an ill-grace that poured its bitterness on Judea. He might be restrained by Rome from occupying Egypt, but he would not be diverted by a small hill-folk from Hellenizing the Orient. Alexander had probably dreamed of a similar project, but he would have sought fusion rather than absorption. If so, his scheme would have been premature. In Alexander's age, Hebraism was not yet well-enough organized to secure its due place in any scheme of fusion. It was fortunate that the attempt was made by a smaller man and at a moment more favourable for resistance. For the task of imposing Hellenism on the East Antiochus IV was not the man, nor was the East then in a receptive condition. Moreover, Hellenism did not win its true victories—throughout the ages it has not won its true victories—in the Seleucid way. The real appeal of Greece has been by charm, not by force, by the lure of its intrinsic beauty, not by compulsion of physical assault. Alexander might have found Hebraism too weak to exercise its proper influence; Antiochus found it too strong to succumb to any other influence. And thus we reach, in the Maccabean age, the most memorable and critical of the Palestinian campaigns. With Egypt decadent but resilient, with Syria pretentious but undermined, with Parthia hostile and Judea roused—while Rome looms on the horizon watchful of all four—we hear the clash which still reverberates in our modern life. To the campaigns associated with the Maccabees I shall turn in my second lecture.

LECTURE II

WARS are often as interesting to the psychologist as to the soldier. Students of character are, in particular, as intrigued by the personalities of the Maccabean campaigns as are military historians by the actual fighting. It is often said that ancient Jewish writers, whether apocalyptics like the author of *Daniel* or sober narrators like the author of the *First Book of the Maccabees*, were unfair to Antiochus Epiphanes. Unfair they were, for they were ignorant of or suppressed his more amiable qualities, yet it is to Polybius the Greek that we owe the fact that Antiochus Epiphanes (the God Manifest) was by the Syrians themselves nicknamed Epimanes (the Madman). It is Polybius who presents the fourth Antiochus to us as a freakish dilettante in the arts, a genial and freakish boon-companion, a statesman, and a buffoon. His practical jokes in the bath roused the wonder and disgust of his courtiers. Antiochus IV the Seleucid reminds us a good deal of William II the Hohenzollern. As Stanley says of Antiochus, his want of balance found expression in 'an eccentricity touching insanity on the left and genius on the right'. There were certainly many attractive features in his disposition. His gallantry as a youth under his father's eyes at Paneion reminds us of the Black Prince under Edward III's observation at Crecy. To the end, as Polybius justly says, and as Daniel confirms, he was skilful in the art of war, though he showed political weakness in his ready surrender to Rome. He was also successful in the arts of peace. During his fifteen years as hostage in Rome, as well as during his stay in Greece, he appears to have won deserved popularity for his amiability, public spirit, and address. Even more to his credit is the fact that on his elevation to the Syrian throne, he practically refounded his capital Antioch, which ultimately played no mean

second role to Alexandria as a social and commercial centre.
' Raum-poesie '—the Poetry of Space—the process of laying out
beautiful cities on sites already beautiful by nature, was an art
in which the successors of Alexander excelled, and Daphne, the
garden suburb of Antioch, is described in terms which befit a
fairy realm.[1] On the other hand, the ambitious design to reduce
the whole of his Empire, including Parthia and Palestine, to a
monotonous uniformity of culture, reveals the megalomaniac as
unmistakably as do his coins, with their mimickings of divinity.
His very attack on Hebraism does not seem to have been,
initially, more than the outcome of overwrought impulse, of
irritation, of self-conceit. Daniel regards his humiliation by
Rome as the cause of his ' indignation against the holy covenant '.
Antiochus made three expeditions into Egypt in the successive
years 170, 169, 168 B.C.; the first was successful, the second
indecisive, the third foiled by Roman intervention. During the
second of these, if we may rely on the *Second Maccabees*, a false
rumour of Antiochus' death led to events in Jerusalem which
the king might easily interpret as a revolt. He had previously
been welcomed by the Jewish Hellenists, and there can be no
doubt that he was encouraged by that welcome in his later
designs. It is not clear how many times Antiochus entered the
Holy City; he did so at least twice and perhaps thrice. On

---

[1] *Poetry of Space.* The term *Raum-poesie* was a happy invention of Burckhardt.
It led to schemes of town-planning far beyond what was reached by us until
very modern times. The new Greek cities were laid out on a regular scheme :
with broad streets intersecting at squares (real squares, not round ones), and at
the centre were the temple and the theatre.   All these new cities were
veritable garden cities ; the gardens were as picturesque as the houses, which is
to say much.   Mahaffy rightly sees in these bright, tasteful cities, full of an
ample and rich life, and connected by good roads, one of the main causes
why Hellenism was so attractive to Jews and Pagans alike.   Jerusalem must
have been very inferior in the respects named not only to Antioch, but also to
the many Hellenic cities within Palestine and on the borders of Judea.
Antiochus deserves considerable credit for his devotion to *Raum-poesie*.
     The craze to-day in America for the *civic centre* is a relic of the Greek Raum-
poesie ; the civic centre in many cases contains in a harmonious group all the
public buildings, from which radiate the main streets in a well-considered
plan.   Our own garden cities and schemes of town-planning are also parallels
to it, and imitations of the Raum-poesie of the period we are considering.

two occasions he despoiled the Temple, and made a savage attack on the inhabitants of Jerusalem. Encouraged by these unopposed successes, he mistook the temper of the people. He imagined that he could win a spiritual as simply as he had won a military triumph. So he ' wrote to his whole nation that they should be one people, and that each should forsake his own laws '. He forgot that neither the true, the good, nor the beautiful is the unique.

This it is that gives to the Maccabean campaigns their special quality. We no longer deal with dynastic struggles, nor with militarist rivalries in which the Jews themselves had little concern. We are faced by a conflict of ideals, each of which has its own inalienable rights, a conflict which has persisted down to our time, and which, incidentally, gave rise to what is termed the Jewish Problem as we know it still, the problem of the relations between citizenship and religion. Much of the literature of the Maccabean age—*Esther, Daniel,* the *Books of the Maccabees*—agrees in representing the struggle as one, not indeed between Hellenism and Hebraism in general, but between Syrian Hellenism and Judean Hebraism. It was a fierce attack on, and an equally fierce defence of, the Jewish Law. I cannot now enter fully into this subject, but the same conclusion may be drawn from the military aspects of the situation. A Ptolemy, a Seleucid, a Roman, were agreed for instance in choosing the Jewish Sabbath for their attacks. Alexander would have been incapable of such tactics. ' I steal no victories ', he exclaimed on a famous occasion. Ptolemy Soter seized Jerusalem on a Saturday ; the Judeans suffered similarly from Antiochus' garrison in the City of David, which made a Saturday raid on the Judean refugees. Mattathias, hearing of this, decided that Jews might carry on a defensive war on the Sabbath day. But this compromise was turned to advantage by Pompey, a century later. He abstained from direct attack on the Saturday, but used the day for raising, unmolested, banks and towers, bringing up his engines into position for a Sunday execution. Clearly, offensive and defensive warfare cannot be discriminated. Other Romans,

Sosius and Titus, took similar advantage, which is justifiable no doubt by military considerations. Plutarch, however, adds insult to injury in his sarcastic comment on one of these incidents. 'God,' writes Plutarch, 'is the brave man's hope, and not the coward's excuse. The Jews indeed once sat on their tails—it being forsooth their Sabbath day—and suffered their enemies to rear their scaling-ladders, and make themselves masters of the walls, and so lay still until they were caught like so many trout in the drag-net of their own superstition.' Generosity to a fallen foe was not an ancient virtue, though Euripides in his *Trojan Women* gives a noble instance to the contrary. In passing, it may be remarked that the weekly day of rest—which modern society regards as one of its most precious of Hebraic institutions —was peculiarly obnoxious to Roman opinion. Nor is it only the satirists like Juvenal that make merry on the matter. Seneca, who should have known better, describes the weekly rest as a pernicious custom, whereby a man by his idleness wastes a seventh part of his life. Yet cowardice was scarcely a trait of the Maccabees, or idleness of the Jews of Nero's age.

It is hard to decide whether it was not, after all, the passive resistance of the Jews that won the real victory. The story of martyrdom is at all events not the least heroic feature of the campaign. When the 'Abomination of Desolation'—with 'its broth of loathèd things'—was set up in Jerusalem, and Dionysiac processions paraded the streets, many conformed under the stress of compulsion. But as Mr. Edwyn Bevan so eloquently and so generously says: 'there also shone out in that intense moment the sterner and sublimer qualities which later Hellenism, and above all the Hellenism of Syria, knew nothing of—uncompromising fidelity to an ideal, endurance raised to the pitch of utter self-devotion, a passionate clinging to purity. They were qualities for the lack of which all the riches of Hellenic culture could not compensate. The agony created new human types, and new forms of literature which became permanent were inherited by Christendom. The figure of the martyr (I am still quoting Mr. Bevan), as the Church knows it, dates from the persecution of Antiochus ; all subsequent martyrologies derive from the Jewish books which record the suffering of those who in that day were strong and did exploits.'

The 'exploits' referred to in this last phrase, quoted from Daniel, must have been the early achievements of the Father of the Maccabees, Mattathias. The moral fortitude of the Mother of the Maccabees, as the medieval Church hymn terms her, who set an example 'merendi perpetuam vitam brevi morte', did not fill the heroic picture. A figure is missing, that of the Son of both, the man who knew both how to live and to die nobly. We turn from Antiochus 'the little horn', to Judas Maccabeus, 'the man of the hammer'. I must leave the discussion of the word Maccabee to a more appropriate occasion. But I do venture to interpolate a suggestion about the 'little horn'. Daniel persistently describes the kings from Alexander onwards as *horns*, and this metaphor is usually explained from the Biblical usage of the horn as a type of strength and arrogance. But I suggest that Daniel was also influenced by the frequency of the horned types on Macedonian and particularly Seleucid coins. It seems strange that no commentator on Daniel has perceived this, even though it has been seen by commentators on the Koran that numismatics account for the appellation 'the two-horned' applied by Arab writers to Alexander.

It was Alexander who introduced the horned types into Greek coinage. On some of his coins are seen two rams' horns curling round his ears. This emblem was adopted in honour of the Egyptian god Ammon, in whose cult the ram was sacred. Horns, with a higher curl, also appear on the Egyptian coins of Alexander to Ptolemy Soter. But it was the founder of the Syrian empire, it was Seleucus, Alexander's cavalry leader, who made the horned type his own. A horned horse's head, and a horned helmet, are characteristic of the Seleucid coinage, and so is the tusked elephant. Hence, I suggest, Daniel's *horns* as types of Alexander and his successors. Perhaps we may here discover the significance of Daniel's '*little* horn' applied to Antiochus IV, perhaps with a note of contempt. The 'little horn' is usually explained to mean 'little in the beginning, though soon increasing in power'. But something fresh is suggested by the coinage. On the later Seleucid coins the horn continues to appear, but it is far smaller than the horns of Alexander's mintage. In a silver tetradrachm of Antiochus IV pictured in Babelon, the small horse's head with yet smaller horns is a mere excrescence to the design; similarly with the tusked elephant: it becomes much reduced in size. ' *Little* horn' may allude to this.

This suggestion of mine is, I fancy, confirmed by another example of what seems to me the influence of coins on metaphors. In the previous century, Theocritus in his Epithalamium compared the rose-red Helen to a mare of Thessalian breed in a chariot; a figure used also by the contemporary author of the *Song of Songs* when praising the Shulammite's loveliness. ' I have likened thee, O my love, to a team of horses in Pharaoh's chariots.' The delicate beauty of the horses on the Sicilian coins—Theocritus was a Sicilian—coins whereon Nikê drives steeds which for grace and refinement are unsurpassed in numismatic art; herein we have a possible explanation for the use by Theocritus (and of his Biblical contemporary) of what may at first sight seem a perverse and grotesque poetical figure. Thus, if I am right, the horned types would not stand alone as a numismatic help to the understanding of ancient poetical imagery.

To return to Judas Maccabeus, there is a feature of his character which even his extreme panegyrists are wont to overlook. Yet Dante saw it. In his *Paradiso* Dante beheld Judas among ' the spirits blessed, who below, ere they came into heaven, were of a great name, so that every Muse would be enriched by them.' In this vision of the Warriors of God, Dante places the Maccabee between Joshua and Charlemagne, a most significant position, reminding us in part of the Pageant of the Nine Worthies, but also suggestive of the thought that while Joshua founded Hebraism in the polity of the ancient world, Charles the Great consolidated the empire of the daughter Church in medieval Europe. But for Judas, Joshua would have been wasted, but for Judas, Charles in a sense impossible. Dante saw the moving wheel of the lofty

Maccabee, and ' gladness was the lash to the top ' : ' e letizia era ferza del paleo '. Whence did Dante derive his ' letizia ' ? Clearly from the Latin version of the *First Maccabees*, where we are told that Judas and his men ' fought with gladness the battle of Israel '—' et proeliabantur proelium Israel cum laetitia '. Dour fighters as the Maccabees were, guilty as they were of cruel barbarities, they possessed the saving quality of cheerfulness. Cromwell's Ironsides droned psalms, the Maccabees accompanied them with the lyre and the dance.

If, however, Judas possessed this quality of ' letizia ' which his panegyrists mostly overlook, he lacked a fault—for it is a fault— which they ascribe to him.   Both Judas and Alexander have been wrongly conceived as merely impetuous assailants of their enemies on the field.   ' He leaped suddenly on the foe,' says the Maccabean historian, and it has been inferred that his successes were due solely to his leonine leaps.   Like Alexander, he had indeed a disinclination to acting on the defensive, but, like Alexander's again, though in a minor degree, his offensive was deliberate : a good deal preceded the leap.   Judas' masterly cam- paigns against the neighbouring tribes, especially in Galilee, prove this ; these were the most brilliant of his successes, rapid sweeps, yet most carefully prepared for.   So, too, was his sudden charge at Emmaus followed a long night march, leading him to the point where he might strike a divided enemy.   There was no sign of a guerrilla chieftain in the prudence which restrained his victory- intoxicated men from disorganized loot—' inasmuch,' said he, ' as there is a battle before us '.   He lacked, however, one of the qualities of a capable leader.   He was weak in commisariat ; more than once he failed to feed his army, a fault which the Syrians, more experienced in the art of war, never committed.   The rest of the qualities Judas possessed.

It is no longer difficult to believe or even to explain his victories over much larger forces.   The last South African War supplied a very close parallel.   The holding of inner lines, the knowledge and choice of ground, added to innate fighting quality and power of endurance, backed by fanatical enthusiasm for their cause, gave the Boers just the same advantages against us as the Judeans enjoyed against the Syrians. The Boers failed for two reasons. First they lacked capacity for bold offensive in the open, and secondly their successes were only won while England was unable to exert her full strength. Judea did not suffer from the first cause ; it did from the second. When, eventually, Syria used her utmost resources, Judea was retaken.

But the real triumph had been won before Judas himself fell at the head of a handful of men on the fatal field of Elasa. Religious liberty had been his true objective, and that objective he attained for all time. Rome might replace Syria as temporal suzerain, but never would the Hebrews surrender their spiritual autonomy. ' Humanly speaking,' writes Mahaffy, ' we may thank Antiochus IV for having saved for us that peculiar Semitic type which has influenced so strongly the literature and politics of the Western world.' Clearly then, we must include the fights of Judas among the ' decisive battles ' of the world.

Yet the victory was secure even before Judas took the field. Just as a gun-shot at Fort Sumter precipitated the American Civil War and sounded the doom of the South, so Mattathias' stroke at Antiochus' commissioner at Modin initiated the Maccabean revolt and ensured its success. Not all the zealots effected forthwith a junction with Mattathias. He and his band made for the open hills, characteristic this of the family daring ; the others sought hiding-places in the caves of the wilderness. It was these others who suffered from the mean attack on the Sabbath day ; it was Mattathias who took steps to prevent a repetition of the manœuvre. Persuaded of his capacity for leadership, the Hasidim thereupon threw in their lot with him, and he made warriors out of scribes. Or rather, his gallant son did this. He did not rely on rude levies, but ' trained his men for service ', says the author of the *Second Maccabees*. In particular he developed the night attack, of which Arrian so strongly disapproved. Night attacks were disastrous in the Boer War, and Arrian's approval of Alexander's abstention from them was just enough. But these unsuccessful night attacks were made by invading troops ignorant of the country; Judas was in another case. His first local successes, won by this device, were so surprising, they were so insistent, that the Syrians were compelled to take serious action.

Accordingly Seron advanced from Samaria, turned east through Lydda, up the same road down which Joshua had chased the Canaanites while the sun stood still on Aijalon. The road between the Beth-horons is rough and steep, and Seron's progress was slow, slower than Judas desired or anticipated. ' We for our part are faint,' moaned his men, ' having tasted no food this day'. So flagrant a lack of rations must have been due to the unexpected deliberation of Seron's approach. ' For our lives and our laws we fight', cried Judas; and the event justified the nobility of his watchword. Attacking the advancing enemy on both sides of the pass, the Judeans threw the Syrians into disorder, from which they could not recover. Two things are clear. Judas lived up to his reputation for taking the offensive, and the Syrians were inefficient in mountain warfare. Indeed the Macedonian tactics, on which the Syrian tactics were based (except that the Syrians used elephants, which Alexander did not), needed level spaces for cavalry skirmishes, supported by the heavy charges of the phalanx. There is no hint that the Syrians modified these dispositions essentially to suit the Judean hills. Alexander, as Arrian tells us, knew how to abandon the rigid phalanx in hill fights, in which he made good use of his bowmen. In a deep, wooded glen Alexander sent on his slingers. We have no indication that the Syrians adopted similar measures; neither bowmen nor slingers are ever mentioned. The Romans, too, were slow to adapt their tactics and formations to meet the lighter Numidians under Hannibal. Curiously enough, while the Syrians, relying on Greek military tradition, were doing the wrong thing for their side, Judas by relying on Hebrew military tradition was doing the right thing for his side. The old Hebrew formations, with their captains of thousands, hundreds, fifties, and tens, the men armed with far lighter weapons than the long and ponderous Syrian sarissa, a spear which prevented its holder from meeting a foe on the flank—this Hebrew formation and armament was far more mobile and agile than the Syrian. The Judeans again were not encumbered by numbers. Numerical superiority, when it goes beyond a usable limit, is by no means an advantage in narrow defiles. Hence Seron was forced to retreat headlong down the hills, and only recovered from the disaster when the open plains were reached.

Antiochus chose this very moment to lead an expedition into Persia, with the object of looting the temple of Artemis in Elymais. Possibly he had his mind set also on recovering Parthia for the Seleucid empire. Hence his attention was distracted from the south. Jerusalem was not the only shrine to be wasted ; Judea not the only part of his dominions in revolt. The edict of Antiochus, enforcing a common religion throughout his realm, must have been as hateful to Zoroastrianism as to Judaism. There was no lack of sympathy with Hellenism in Persia, but the religion of Persia resented suppression at the *mot d'ordre* of a Seleucid. Later on, that other stronghold of Zoroastrianism, Parthia, long held out against Rome. Eventually, Zoroastrianism fell an easy prey to Islam, with which it had close affinity. In the almost concurrent opposition to Syrian pseudo-Hellenism by Parthia and Judea may be detected a spiritual as well as a political coincidence. Tacitus, blind to the importance of the Judean revolt, is right in his judgement that Antiochus' distraction between north and south gave the Maccabees their chance. Strange is it to contrast Polybius with the *Books of the Maccabees.* According to Jewish sources, the death of Antiochus was a divine retribution for his defilement of the Temple of Jerusalem. According to Polybius, his fate was due to manifestations of divine wrath in the course of his wicked attempt on the temple of Elymais. After all, the two versions are not inconsistent. Antiochus showed the same spirit in both cases.

Antiochus conducted the northern campaign in person, because there was more chance of rich booty. He was in financial difficulties, and the Persian temples had hitherto been spared. So far from having been robbed by former invaders, former invaders had added to the rich stores of precious metals in Elymais and elsewhere. On the other hand, Antiochus himself had already despoiled Jerusalem, and little more could be extorted from it. Indeed his generals merely hoped to obtain money from the Judean campaigns by selling their anticipated prisoners as slaves. For this reason, though we can well imagine that he would have preferred to proceed himself against the upstart Judas, Antiochus relegated the conduct of the Judean campaign to his viceroy Lysias. Lysias had some attractive qualities; in the end he yielded religious liberty like a gallant gentleman, while in the meantime campaigning like an expert soldier. We shall not now follow in detail the proceedings of Lysias' two generals, Nicanor and Gorgias. But one detail is interesting. I have already referred to it. With the new Syrian army came a group of coast slave-dealers, provided with cash and fetters. Slave-dealing was a regular item of Phoenician trade, and the Syrians conceived that, as the price of Israelites taken and sold, they might extract from these dealers money enough to pay the over-due Roman tribute. It was Nicanor who originated this amiable idea, bearing, as one of our sources says, ' a deadly hatred unto Israel ', and exciting a similar animosity in return. The bitter-ness was accentuated by the fact, if it be a fact, that Nicanor at first was well enough disposed to Judas, but the latter, fearing treachery, refused to second his friendly advances. At all events, the overthrow of Nicanor is treated by the *Second Maccabees* as a retaliation for his dastardly attempt to enslave a people. When Nicanor, three years later, was finally conquered and slain by Judas, in 161 B. C., Nicanor's Day, the anniversary of his fall, was observed as a public holiday, every thirteenth of Adar.

But we must return to the earlier trial of strength between Nicanor and Judas. In association with Gorgias, Nicanor was commissioned to make the attempt at which Seron had failed, and to overwhelm the forces led by Judas. After his victory over Seron, Judas must have hovered on the Judean hills, watching an opportunity to re-enter Jerusalem. That city was strongly held by the Syrians, and attracted not only Judas, but also the Syrian invaders. The persistent marches of the Syrians to Jerusalem as an objective, while the Judeans were *not* in occupation of Jerusalem, must have been caused by two thoughts : first, that Judas and his men would be caught on the way ; second, that Jerusalem was a good centre for combing out the rebels in the Judean hills and wadys. I demonstrated this in my own visit to Judea, made for the purpose of carefully going over on foot all the scenes of the Maccabean campaigns. I found that by making Jerusalem a centre I could cross and recross all Judea, while never being more than some twelve hours distant from the Holy City.

To return to the fight between Judas and Lysias' generals, Nicanor and Gorgias. This I interpret as a combing-out process. I find it hard to understand it in any other way. Gorgias was a better soldier than his colleague Nicanor, and was scarcely involved in that colleague's defeat. He does not seem to have been in Nicanor's camp at all, but to have moved westwards from Jerusalem while Nicanor advanced eastwards from the coast, on the very lines followed by Richard I in his march from Acre nearly fourteen centuries later. Nicanor encamped his main forces on the lower slopes, for the hills on the Jaffa road have hardly begun when Emmaus is reached. It was at Emmaus that he awaited Judas' expected attack, though he also undertook an initiative of his own, by arranging for Gorgias' concentration. He had learned his lesson from Seron's fate, and declined to entangle himself in the hill passes. He held at Emmaus an ample ground for using his cavalry and phalanx, while the flanking movement of Georgias coming from Jerusalem would compel Judas to attack on the site chosen by the Syrians. The best view of what followed is that the Syrian plan failed because of Judas' rapidity and resource. He actually marched in front of Gorgias and on the same road, covered at a great pace the twenty miles between Mizpah and Emmaus, rested his troops overnight, and then, looking over the hills, and catching a glimpse of the Syrian camp facing east, 'showed himself in the plain' as soon as it was dawn. This is a fine touch. As the modern traveller approaches Emmaus by Judas' route, the plain of Emmaus does indeed come suddenly into view. Emmaus was a very different affair to Beth-horon. Here below lay a ramparted, well-patrolled camp, showing in the morning light. If Judas' attack was a surprise, surprise was not the whole explanation of the Syrian panic. Judas, in light formation, attacked on the south, while Nicanor expected him from the east or north. Now on the south the ground is broken and steep, ill-suited to Syrian battle tactics. Nicanor had, moreover, encamped too near the hills, as is indicated by the statement that after the morning panic he ' fled to the plain '. The pursuit was not driven home. Yet Judas' anxiety as to the oncoming of Gorgias was wasted. Seeing what had occurred to Nicanor, Gorgias declined the battle, which Judas on the lower ground was unable to compel. Gorgias either retraced his steps to Jerusalem or withdrew south-west to Azotus. I would only remark that in the view here taken of the Battle of Emmaus, Gorgias did not lose his way in a night-march, but failed to catch up with Judas until too late to help Nicanor.

Signal as was Judas' victory at Emmaus, Jerusalem was still barred to him. He could not venture on entering the city while the Syrians held the citadel, and might be succoured by another Syrian advance from the plain. It needed a third victory to so assure himself of the latter point as to risk entering the Holy City. In 165 B.C., a year glorious in the annals of Judea, and indeed of the world, this third victory arrived, at Bethzur. Lysias himself led a large army into Judea—far too large. The Syrians, throughout, would have had a better chance with smaller forces. Mass or shock attacks, in which the formidable phalanx could operate, were impossible in Judea. So, too, the hand-to-hand combats of olden times were not helped by numbers in the moment of battle, while mere numbers were detrimental on marches and still more so in retreats. Panic mostly seized those who, in the rear, were taking no part in the actual fighting, and their panic reacted on the fighting line.

Lysias abandoned the northern passes and lower ranges which had proved disastrous to Seron and Nicanor. He advanced possibly through Beersheba and thence, after a long Idumean detour, from the south by the Hebron road. Allenby used this very road, but he also used the Beth-horon route, as we shall see. Returning to Lysias, we now hear of the elephants for the first time, and naturally. Even the Syrians would have shrunk from trying to bring up elephants by any other approach than the comparatively broad and level Hebron road. The first thing that struck me on the site of Beth Zacharias was that here was a very suitable ground for an elephant-led assault. The Syrians and Egyptians were great believers in elephants; the Romans, after much perturbation, eventually proved that these beasts were more dangerous to friend than foe. It has been objected that the Jewish sources are unhistoric in their references to Antiochus IV's elephants, seeing that by the treaty with Rome, a quarter of a century earlier, Antiochus III had contracted to discontinue the use of elephants. But such agreements are soon broken. We have a similar case with the Gallic horses. The Romans imposed conditions on the Gauls with regard to the breeding of horses which very soon were modified. To clinch the matter—before the Roman legates arrived !—Polybius himself records the presence of a large number of elephants in the great festival celebrated by Antiochus IV in his capital.

Here again the facts are dead against certain critics. For we are told in 1 Macc. iii. 34 that while only a part of the Syrian army was employed in Judea, all the elephants were so used in 163 B.C. Further on, in 1 Macc. vi. 30, we are told that thirty-two elephants were used in Judea. This agrees with Polybius, who (in the procession at Antioch in 165 B.C.), in addition to a few chariot elephants, describes the presence of 'thirty-six elephants in single file with all their furniture on '. The coincidence of numbers is almost exact.

These elephants were of value chiefly against other elephants. Polybius gives us a spirited account of the superiority of the Indian elephants (used by the Syrians) to the African variety (used by the Egyptians). Not only the soldiers in the howdahs fought, but the elephants themselves engaged in the conflict, pushing each other forehead to forehead, until one or other prevailed, turned aside its rival's trunk, and so got a chance to ' pierce his rival with his tusks as a bull would with his horns'. The smaller Lybian elephants gave way in this manner before the bigger Indian beasts at Raphia, afraid, says Polybius, of their size and their trumpetings and smell.

The Romans, as Polybius also records, stood in great terror of the Carthaginian elephants, until they learned how to deal with them.[1] The Judeans had no such fear as the Romans, but from the first faced the elephants with extraordinary daring. They were not for a moment perturbed by Lysias' elephants—even though they were excited by being shown ' the blood of grapes and mulberries '. Why ?

Lysias then with his men and elephants marched round Judas' flank and rear, hoping to catch him between his own troops and the hostile Idumeans. But Judas was not at Lysias' mercy. His former successes had given him more than fame. He now had an army, with arms captured from Nicanor. Lysias was forced to retreat, felt the impossibility of continuing the struggle against Judas, and left the road to Jerusalem open. Judas took the opportunity, rededicated the Temple amidst a scene of joyous triumph, raised fortifications against the citadel still held by a well-provisioned Syrian garrison, fortified Bethzur, and entered on the most brilliant of his exploits, the campaign in Galilee.

But we cannot now follow those events closely. Judas was to win other victories, but it would seem that his popularity was waning. The people on the whole were content with what had been won, and when Bacchides four years after the rededication of the Temple met Judas at Elasa, the Maccabee was supported by a mere handful of die-hards. Whether this was because of the unpopularity of Judas' political designs, or because Bacchides caught him for once unawares, Judas fell ; but he had not fought in vain. The Syrians henceforth sought to conciliate, not to

---

[1] As alarmed as Germans at the first sight of ' tanks.'

conquer, Judea. Hebraism had been saved, and the event was confirmed by royal proclamation. The most momentous of the Palestinian campaigns was the most successful in its issues for humanity.

One of Judas' last acts was to send an embassage to Rome. The authenticity of this embassage is now generally admitted by historians. Mommsen suggests that Rome assented to the recognition of Jewish autonomy because it desired to establish a buffer state between Egypt and Syria. For the first time since Solomon, the Jews controlled the coast. On the Maccabean mausoleum at Modin were engraved realistic figures of ships, typifying the fact that Judea at last was a naval power. Rome had something very definite to gain from an alliance. This continued for a century, until first Syria and then Egypt was completely Romanized. When Rome controlled *both* Syria and Egypt, Judea was no longer needed as a buffer state, and the fate of a useless buffer state was annihilation or absorption.

It was Pompey who, in 63 B.C., practically reduced Judea to a Roman province. Pompey advanced on Jerusalem from the north, by the east of the Jordan. He crossed that river near Scythopolis, thence entered Judea, and occupied Jerusalem without a blow. But the Temple itself was defended, and the defended Temple was a formidable fortress, as Titus found. Like Titus, Pompey assaulted the Temple from the north and west, the only sides vulnerable to ancient instruments of war. A massacre of priests followed, while far more disastrously the coast towns from Raphia to Dora, and the Hellenic cities fringing Judea east and west of the Jordan, were freed from Judean authority. The Judean king Aristobulus walked in front of the conqueror's chariot when in 61 B.C. Pompey celebrated his triumph at Rome. And though Pompey introduced no fundamental change in the internal government of Judea proper, the country was henceforth vassal to Rome.

But Rome could never undo what the Maccabees had achieved. No Roman Emperor was ever deified in Jerusalem, and in Rome itself the pinch of incense implored at pagan shrines was refused

by the early Christians.   Rome, entering into the legacy of
Hellenism, found, in Mommsen's words, that the world was under
two masters.   And this was well.   Under a single master the
world is never safe.   The campaigns which we have surveyed
to-day were, at least in part, responsible for the fact that the
world emerged into the Christian era with two masters, not with
one ; with God enthroned as well as Caesar.

LECTURE III

IF a military expert had been addressing you,you would probably have often heard from his lips the terms 'strategy' and 'tactics'. Approaching as I now do the campaign of Vespasian and Titus, I feel impelled to use these technical words for once. Strategy is (I learn from the *Oxford Dictionary*) the higher leadership, the direction of campaigns, while tactics is the art of handling troops in the immediate presence of the enemy ; strategy is the comprehensive plan, tactics the detailed execution. The Romans excelled the Judeans in strategy, the Judeans surpassed the Romans in tactics. In general it may be said that the Judeans were better tacticians than strategists ; they allowed, for instance, the Romans to hem them into Jerusalem, but having made this strategic blunder, they showed a tactical ingenuity and strength that almost compensated for their strategic weakness.

In reading Josephus' vivid narrative of Titus' siege of the Holy City, one knows not whether to wonder more at the resourcefulness of the defenders or the conventionality of the assailants. In Dion Cassius' account, the Roman infantry was not always steady, but deserted to their enemy in the course of the operations. We must naturally allow for the difference in spirit in the opposing forces ; the legionaries had not the same impulse to attack as the Zealots to defend. But it is Titus' tactics that seem to lack genius. He was prompt enough in countering the Judean devices after they had done their damage ; he showed less foresight in anticipating them. The attack was made by rule ; the defence broke through all rules. Had there been union within the walls, Titus, even with the aid of famine, could hardly have taken the city without heavy reinforcements, and Rome could not have supplied them. As it was, considerable movements of troops were necessary in order to provide the three legions which Titus commanded.

A curious parallel between the campaign of Titus and that of Allenby may be noted in this connexion. During the last phase of the Great War, the exigences of the Western Front necessitated a transference of troops between Palestine and Europe. A similar incident occurred in the first century A. D. Two of the legions usually serving in Syria had been dispatched to the Caspian, but the outbreak of the Judean revolt forced the Romans to hurry these legions back to Egypt. Thence Titus led them to join Vespasian at Ptolemais in the beginning of 67; thus bringing Vespasian's Judean army to a total of three legions. To replace the two transferred legions, Nero moved troops from Britain, the legion so moved wintering in Rome, where the disturbed condition of affairs rendered its presence opportune. This is by no means the only instance of Britain reacting to events in Judea. Julius Severus, Hadrian's legate, was actually summoned from Britain to Judea to act against Bar Cochba, and the record of Julius' subsequent triumph mentions on one and the same inscription his services in Britain and in Judea. When we add the heroic part played by English princes in the Crusades, which strangely enough reverberated in the Crimean War, it is no new departure for this country to have a unique concern in the care of the Holy Land. At former times England participated in Palestinian wars ; its Mandate now is of Peace.

The Roman campaign which ended in the destruction of the Temple and City of Jerusalem in A. D. 70 is usually pronounced inevitable. That problem is really more in need of discussion than the actual campaign itself. No martial episode has ever been described with more graphic power and pathetic particularity. In his history of this campaign Josephus proves himself a master of style. It must suffice to say that Titus marched from the north-west, and encamped on the north-east and west of Jerusalem, thus controlling the approaches on all sides but the south. This we may assume was also strongly patrolled, for, though the historians omit all mention of Roman operations to the south of

the city, they are equally silent as to any attempt to relieve or
provision the city from the Hebron direction. With his wings
resting on Antonia and the upper city, Titus was in a position to
attack the Temple from the north to the south-west of that
fortified edifice. All this was well planned, better planned than
any previous siege. There was only one better plan possible,
and that was Allenby's. The British General succeeded in
manœuvring the Turks out of Jerusalem without firing a single
shot at the hallowed precincts. Titus' plan, then, was good
enough; the conduct of the siege was less efficient. But the
terrible end came, as Josephus records it, and we may draw a
veil over the grim story. The end, due to dissension within as
much as to prowess without, was indeed inevitable. But though,
under the prevailing conditions, the end was inevitable, it is not
so certain that the beginning could not have been avoided. It is
not an easy question. Josephus clearly was a pacifist, but his
opposition to the revolt was based on a wise foresight. ' I perceived that we were on the eve of war,' he tells us in his Auto-
biography; 'I saw that many were elated at the idea'. He
pleaded for peace. ' I desired them to refrain from rashly risking
the most terrible woes for their country, their families, and themselves. This I urged with eager exhortation, for I foresaw that
the end of the war would be most unfortunate for us. But I
could not persuade them, for the madness of desperate men
carried the day.' Very unjustly as it seems to me, Josephus has
been censured for a lack of patriotism, because he feared that the
firebrands were more likely to injure Judea than Rome. Josephus'
faults are beyond defence, but lack of patriotism was not one of
them. In real patriotism, loyalty to his people's spirit, and pride
in its institutions, no one, not even Philo, ranks higher.

Josephus wrote not only a history of the Jews but an apologia
for Judaism which has stood the test of centuries as a sincere
constructive effort. Seeing the cause of the revolt in the
stupidity of Florus, Josephus thought that a different governor
to Florus might make Roman government tolerable. According
to Suetonius the cause of the revolt lay deeper. He speaks of

the belief then current throughout the East that in Judea were to arise masters of the world. This, says he, referred to Rome as the event proved; but the Jews applied it to themselves. Such a belief Josephus, too, would have regarded as fulfilled when Vespasian was nominated as emperor on Judean soil. Nor did Josephus stand alone in such an interpretation. Johanan, son of Zakkai, is said in a Jewish source to have prophesied Vespasian's imperial destiny just as Josephus did. Now Johanan was a foremost leader to the Pharisees, and he, no more than Josephus, advocated war with Rome. 'Ye fools!' he cried to the war-party within Jerusalem, 'why seek ye to destroy the city and burn the Temple?' This is almost identical language to that used by Josephus.

So, as the story goes, Johanan escaped from the city in a coffin, and in Jamnia, as the facts go, he, during the war, refounded Judaism like a second Ezra. Thus these two foremost men, Josephus and Johanan, otherwise superficially dissimilar, the statesman and the Rabbi, agreed in their desire to make terms with Vespasian, and in their estimates of state and Temple on one side and of what state and Temple enshrined on the other. Johanan stands above Josephus in his abhorrence of war, as became a disciple of that gentle-hearted peace-lover Hillel, but Josephus as little as Johanan thought this particular war inevitable. No war, I submit, is inevitable, except to those who are determined *not* to avoid it. Unluckily, though it takes two sides to make a peace, one side is enough to make a war.

The full consequences of the catastrophe engineered by Vespasian and Titus were not felt for half a century, when Bar Cochba failed in his bold effort to undo it under Hadrian. Until that failure, the hope of recovery was so vivid that the point of the catastrophe was covered if not blunted. 'Iudaea devicta' of the Roman coins belongs in date to 70, but in effect to 135. Yet important as was the campaign of which Bar Cochba was hero, Dion Cassius probably exaggerates its military significance, though it was significant enough for Rome to use its greatest general and to place four legions under his command. Simon bar Cochba figures in Jewish legend as a true superman, of gigantic physical and messianic power.[1]

Bar Cochba's revolt was the aftermath of Jewish insurrections in Greece, Cyprus, and Egypt at the end of Trajan's reign (A.D. 114-117). As the papyri now fully attest, Trajan was much troubled by rival complaints of each other by the worshippers of Jehovah and Serapis. Wordy arguments led to more tragic encounters, and throughout the Orient at the beginning of the second century A.D. we are confronted by fierce triumphs by Jews, countered by yet more ferocious retaliations. As to the extent of these atrocities in the Diaspora on both sides, Dion exaggerates. Similarly he elevates the Palestinian revolt of Bar Cochba under Hadrian into a world-movement. Dr. Büchler has made it certain that Bar Cochba's insurrection was local and restricted to Judea. What may have misled Dion is the fact that Hadrian's consent to the rebuilding of the Temple was a matter in which the Jews of the Diaspora were all interested. There is no basis for the statement that Rabbi Akiba's travels were designed to excite the Jews outside Palestine to participate in Bar Cochba's movement. The Diaspora had no concern in the revolt, which, however, may have arisen out of the disappointment when Hadrian's disposition towards rebuilding the Temple changed from favour to opposition. Instead of reviving a Jewish home in Jerusalem, Hadrian converted the city into a Roman centre, Aelia Capitolina, with a new temple dedicated to the Capitoline Jupiter. According to Dion, this was indeed the immediate cause of the rising. At first the

---

[1] Very remarkable is the fact that Akiba accepted Bar Cochba as Messiah, though no claim was made by him to Davidic descent. Krauss's statement that the older Nizzahon records Bar Cochba's Davidic lineage is unfounded. The Nizzahon simply infers the fact on argumentative grounds: 'It would seem', says that authority, 'that Ben Koziba who reigned in Bethar was of the family of David, for lo! he said, I am Messiah! and the Sages did not retort on him: Thou art not of the House of David'. Thus the Nizzahon has not even a tradition of Bar Cochba's Davidic descent; it is only a medieval inference of no historical importance. We have a parallel with Las Casas and Napoleon. For long the former devotee to the Bourbons refused to accept the latter as rightful emperor. He explained his change of mind to Napoleon in the words: 'I was conquered by your glory.' The same may have happened to Akiba with regard to Bar Cochba. He was conquered by his glory.

result was literally subterranean ; in modern phrase, the Judeans dug themselves in, occupying a series of caverns interconnected by trenches. At first contemptuous, the Romans (so Dion asserts) were roused to energy when they realized that the movement was spreading out of these holes to dimensions coterminous with the inhabited world. He adds the interesting detail that non-Jewish sympathizers joined the revolutionary ranks. This reminds us of the Foreign Legions in modern wars, though in Hadrian's day the attraction was hope of booty, not, as in our times, love of adventure. On the other hand, if non-Jews joined Bar Cochba, the Jewish-Christians were less compliant. Justin Martyr informs us (and as a contemporary he was in a position to know) that the Christians in Palestine refused to throw in their lot with the Jews against Rome. In this fact we may detect the actual separation of Church from Synagogue. If so, Bar Cochba's campaign, without attaining the military dimensions ascribed to it, was of the utmost import for the future.

There is only one other point to which I would now call your attention before passing on. Dion states that more than half-a-million Jews fell in the Bar Cochba War, and this exclusive of those who died from privation and disease. This must be pure legend. In fact the whole story of Bar Cochba is full of such mythical embellishments, and when in his novel *Son of a Star* Richardson conveyed Bar Cochba to Ireland, where he lived happy ever afterwards, he was keeping pace with the older fairy-tales regarding that hero. Thus the Seder Olam assert that the war lasted three-and-a-half years. This is too reminiscent of the three-and-a-half years of Daniel and the Maccabees. Yet I dare say it could be made out that the recent Palestinian campaign also lasted exactly three-and-a-half years. Legend and fact do often kiss each other. But the important point regarding Dion's huge estimate of the Jewish casualties between A.D. 131 and 135 is this. If Josephus' numbers of those who perished in 70 be true, how did Judea recover in the interval sufficiently to provide such immense forces for Bar Cochba? In other words, we must gravely distrust the *numbers* given by classical and other ancient historians. It may be doubted whether very large armies ever faced each other in the field until the American Civil War. In that war the numbers engaged on both sides reached unprecedented proportions. Similarly, it may be questioned whether ancient deportations ever equalled the numbers attained by the removals of Greeks which have recently occurred, or have been contemplated.

Hadrian drew the plough over the Temple hill, founded his brand-new Aelia Capitolina, and wrote *finis* over the ruins of Jerusalem. But destiny laughs at short-sighted finalities, and while Aelia Capitolina as a name for Jerusalem is known only to antiquaries, Jerusalem is the name which it continued to bear. So far from remaining a pagan city, Jerusalem the Holy, or el-Kuds, was destined to be a meeting-place of the daughter faiths born out of Judaism—too often the battle-place of children fighting over their mother's grave. But there was a noble side to the struggle after Constantine had erected his basilica and Omar his mosque. Jerusalem became the object of pious veneration to others besides St. Helena, and the possession of the Holy Land thenceforward changed into an ideal in and for itself. This is by no means true throughout the Middle Ages, but it is true enough to differentiate the newer from the older Palestinian campaigns. The older campaigns had for the most part been motivated by everything but love for the land itself. Under Byzantine rule, such love was strongly developed. The new feeling was intensified by the Moslem conquest. In between, the Persians under Chosroes had again sacked Jerusalem—this was in 614, so that what little of the city had persisted under the Byzantines had long vanished when Saladin came into possession. As a result of the many sieges, nearly all of the ancient city now lies deep underground.

Thus the desolation of Palestine preceded and did not follow the Crusades ; the latter had their share in the devastation, but they were not solely responsible for it. To the Jewish inhabitants, the Crusading era was an era of severe trial, but so were previous eras, if to a lesser degree. The Arab conquest of Egypt occurred in 639, when Amr, anticipating Nelson's contrivance under a like contingency, turned a blind eye to his master's recall. The victory of the Arabs at the Yarmuk in 636 settled the fate of Western Palestine for several centuries. It is curious to note that at the siege of Beisan which followed the fight at the Yarmuk, the Byzantines held up the Moslem advance for a whole winter by flooding the marshes with Jordan water— a device which proved so serviceable in saving Calais in the first winter of the Great War. The Byzantines threw away their advantage, advanced beyond the marshes which gave them safety, suffered a complete rout, and left the Moslems with an open road to Jerusalem. Then we come upon a medieval analogue to the Palestinian conditions during the struggles of Ptolemies and Seleucids. Again rivalries between Egypt and Syria for central authority in Islam threw Palestine not only into the hands of regular armies, but also of marauding bands independent alike of both Syria and Egypt.

As to the effects of all these countless conflicts from the tenth to the twelfth century on the internal condition of Palestine, much new information is now available. This new information comes from Egypt, and if it is not as gorgeous as Lord Carnarvon's sensational discoveries in the Valley of the Kings at Thebes, it is coloured by an interest of its own. This new information derives from Hebrew documents of the Cairo Geniza, now in Cambridge, and several students, notably Dr. Jacob Mann, have printed and annotated the documents. Future historians of Medieval Palestine will find here much to add that was previously unknown, and means of giving greater vividness to what was known already. These Hebrew documents describe the events at an angle different to that from which the Christian and Moslem sources regard them, and thus the first supplements the other two. The tramp of armies as of yore is heard along the Palestinian littoral, but for the first time we have full records of the economic and the social, as distinct from the military, results of the campaigns. I felt bound to allude to this new information, but I can do no more than allude to it to-day. Dr. Mann has certainly empowered historians to envisage more definitely than before the exact condition of Palestine at the outbreak of the first Crusade. In particular he shows us the horror and the glory of the Levantine piracy. Cargoes of enslaved Jews and Christians were carried by Saracenic corsairs from Byzantine ships. If this piracy was the curse of the age, the method of dealing with it by generous ransomers may be set down on the scroll of honour.

Regarded from their most serious aspect, the Crusaders merely continued on a large scale the conditions which, on a smaller scale, had long established themselves. Before the Crusades, we see men of little ability for war or peace seeking power at the end of lance or scimitar, and dying by the weapons by which they sought to live. The Crusaders were abler and stronger, but they too, on their route to the olden home of the Jews, massacred Jewish congregations in Europe, and when they reached their goal helped to complete the ruin of the Jewish communities in Palestine. But the idealism of the Crusading impulse was not, as some historians contend, altogether smirched by the realism of what actually occurred. This idealism is apparent from the first march of peasants and princes under Godfrey in 1026 to the very last of its series some three centuries later. The Crusading impulse was no ephemeral emotion. One of the first things that strikes the student of the Crusading records is the slow deliberation with which the armies moved. These delays were of themselves tests of sincerity: an enthusiasm that so endures must be deep-seated. Some fell out by the way, others (if the pun be allowed) fell out with each other. But, as Archer truly says: The Crusades 'were primarily wars of an idea', under the inspiration of which (despite lower motives) the Crusaders ventured their lives. The results of the Crusades are hard to gauge, but they assuredly formed a true and sound link in that intercourse of East and West which has recurrently influenced civilization, while the travellers and geographers of the epoch prepared the way for Columbus and Vasco da Gama. 'Economically and socially', writes Joseph Jacobs, 'the Crusades were disastrous to the European Jews'; they did not recover from their effects till the end of the eighteenth century. But this much must, I think, be added : if they gave us a fanatic Randulph, they produced also a Bernard of Clairvaux.

From the military standpoint, we might assert that the Crusades are a footnote to Mahan's theory of sea-power. The possession of the coast was essential, yet Saladin, who had it not, was left unconquered by Richard I, who had it. Saladin suffered much because of his failure to take Acre before Richard's arrival.

This failure to take Acre would have been decisive against Saladin but for an ally more powerful than all the reinforcements which Cairo or Damascus could have sent to Saladin's aid. This ally was malaria. Richard I had no sooner landed at Acre than he was attacked by the disease, and later, at the last critical moment when he could have won the war at a stroke, he was again incapacitated by the same disease. General Allenby's army suffered considerably from the disease. Much changes with time : thus Allenby could reach Jerusalem from Cairo by motor-car. But the malaria had remained. The whole of this subject of malaria and Palestinian wars deserves fuller treatment, but without a bare mention of it my account of Palestinian campaigns would have been even more hopelessly incomplete than it is.

To return, Saladin succeeded in the end, though he had lost the command of the coast.

On the other hand, the Crusades failed on the whole because they relied too much on the mastery of the sea. As Sir Mark Sykes well says : 'Because the Moslems lost command of the sea, the Crusades were possible ; but a power based solely on sea-power cannot penetrate far into a continent where (as in the case of Asia Minor) the valleys run parallel to the littoral. The Crusaders held the coast, but never established themselves in the strategic centre of what should have been their Empire.' To military historians this is all-important, to other students a more human factor emerges. This factor is the revelation of personalities.

It is this factor that makes the Third Crusade the most fascinating of the series. And this is true, though the First gained, while the Third failed to gain its objective—Jerusalem. The First Crusade took Jerusalem from a divided Moslem power: Richard I had to face in the Third Crusade a united Islam led by a consummate ruler of men. Indeed the Third Crusade was unique, not merely in its own series, but in the whole series of Palestinian campaigns. Others of these campaigns produced great leaders—an Alexander, a Judas, a Pompey, a Napoleon, an Allenby. But in none of these instances was there a rival fit to face him. Napoleon was not opposed in Palestine to a Wellington. It is true that ultimately Napoleon was foiled by Nelson and the Nile, which was fought while the Emperor was in Egypt, about to advance into Palestine. But Napoleon's actual defeat in Palestine was due to a much lesser man. In the Third Crusade, on the contrary, the duel was fought by rivals worthy of each other. Despite the faults of both, Richard of the Lion-Heart and Saladin Defender of the Faith outstand as types of chivalry and subtlety. Both were capable of savage atrocities, both of generous humanities. The finer soldier was Richard. Saladin could beat a Raymond at Hattin, near Tiberias, in 1187, but he was no match for Richard at Arsuf, near Jaffa, in 1191. Saladin, however, was successful where Richard was a failure—in maintaining union within his own camp. Throughout his many and vast campaigns, Saladin was loyally supported, winning this fidelity by his sweetness of temper. Richard, besides the ravages of sickness, was thwarted by the infidelities of allies; in part he owed the disloyalty to his arrogant disposition. Stubbs, like so many moderns, is inclined to exalt Saladin at the expense of Richard, holding also that the Moslem should be judged by a more lenient standard. 'Saladin', says Stubbs, 'was a good heathen, Richard a bad Christian; set side by side there is not much to choose between them; judged each by his own standard, there is very much.' But we cannot consent to estimate values by this method, for it is based on a prejudiced estimate of the standards themselves. For myself, my sympathy goes out to Richard, great alike in his high hopes, great in his disillusionment. Noble souls do not react to similar experiences in similar ways. Moses, agaze on Pisgah, steadily views the Promised Land which he is never to enter. Richard, within seeing-distance of the Holy City, whose streets he must not tread, turns his head away. Heroic both, he of the steady gaze, and he of the eyes averted!

The Crusades were, as Stubbs rightly says, 'caused by a movement as religious as the Reformation, and much less connected with political objects'. The Palestinian campaigns that followed them were not so distinguished; they were either predatory raids or moves in the political game. Such was the case with the Mongol invasions and with Selim's campaign in 1516, when he wrested the country from the Mamelukes, and incorporated it in the Turkish Empire, in which it remained, with a short interval, until the coming of Allenby. Selim, 'finding the (last) Abbasid Caliph cowering in Cairo, bought the title, robe, and office from him for his (own) heirs and successors'. And in Selim's family the Caliphate still remains, even after the recent Angora *coup de main*.

There were rumours of campaigns animated by less political designs. The trade of Smyrna had declined with the growth of Constantinople; but, in the first half of the seventeenth century Smyrna rose into new commercial prominence during the war between Turkey and Venice. It then became the centre of the Levantine trade, English houses established branches there, and a certain Mordecai Zebi was employed as agent by one of these English firms. Mordecai was thus well informed as to the dreams of the Fifth Monarchy men, in London, while people in London heard all about the doings at Smyrna. It is therefore from English correspondence that we hear most of the man who threatened to lead a new Crusade—this time a Jewish Crusade. Here again English interest in Palestine reveals itself. The Fifth Monarchy men expected the Messianic year in 1666, and Sabbathai the son of Mordecai Zebi was hailed by others besides his deluded brethren-in-faith as the destined redeemer, who would overthrow the Sultan and, riding on a lion with a seven-headed dragon as its reins, would lead back the tribes to the Holy Land.

' Believers in London,' as Graetz expresses it, ' in English fashion
offered odds of 10 to 1 that Sabbathai would be appointed King
at Jerusalem within the year, and drew formal bills of exchange
upon the issue '. It is to Sabbathai's credit that his campaign
was never conceived in militarist terms. Unlike the dreams of
an Alroy or similar figures of history or myth who play the role
of Jewish conquerors of the Holy Land—Sabbathai's visions
were bloodless. His weapons were to be the magic mystery of
the Sacred Name, and the charming power of music ; on pageantry
he relied more than on panoply of arms. His excited followers
wound up their affairs, got ready their household goods, not their
swords. They conceived not a campaign, but an emigration.
The end of all these ecstasies was disillusion : Sabbathai was not
of the stuff of which heroes are made.

If there was scarcely any political colour to Sabbathai's dreams,
there was nothing but political colour to Napoleon's, a century
later. Napoleon's motives for marching from Cairo to Acre were
magnified by him, in St. Helena, into gigantic purposes of Asiatic
(including Indian) dominion. Certainly he masqueraded as the
saviour of Islam, and, amid the ribald laughter of his troopers at
the pantomime, associated himself with Mohammedan ritual. He
proclaimed himself a Crusader of the Crescent, if the paradox be
permissible. In point of fact his true intentions (proclaimed by
him in February, 1799, immediately before leaving Cairo) were
three : (1) to consolidate his hold on Egypt—for Napoleon felt that
to hold Egypt it is necessary to hold Palestine also ; (2) to deprive
England of Syrian bases ; and (3) to overawe Turkey. Up to
the Battle of the Nile, Turkey had shown indecision between
alliance with England or with France. Turkey has always been
moved by events of the hour ; her very indecision has been the
secret of her resilience. Just as Turkey recently joined Germany
because the *Goeben* reached Constantinople, so she joined England
in 1799 because of the victory of Nelson. Napoleon's Egyptian
campaign was ruined by this interruption of sea-communications
with France. Napoleon had started for Palestine, and his troops
were in the desert, before he heard of the Nile. He marched by

the usual route, through el-Arish to Gaza, Jaffa, Acre. At Acre his advance was finally checked by the resource of that extraordinary sailor, Sidney Smith. Nelson had no high opinion of him, while Napoleon called him a young fool and a captain of brulôts. But Smith surprised both Nelson and Napoleon, and by his skilful handling of his small naval force compelled Napoleon to raise the siege of Acre after sixty-two days of vain investment. Reviewing the episode at St. Helena, Napoleon dated his fall, not from his retreat from Moscow, but from his failure at Acre.

We pass to the last stage of our long journey. Would it have been necessary but for the penultimate stage? In 1831 Ibrahim Pasha advanced from Alexandria, took Acre in 1832, and annexed Palestine to Egypt. England again intervened, and the guns of Napier's fleet restored the country to Turkey. The course of the Great War would, in part at least, have been radically different had Palestine remained under Egyptian control when England took charge of Egypt after Arabi Pasha's rising in 1882. Had not England in 1840 given Palestine back to Turkey, Allenby's campaign might have been unnecessary.

But it was necessary. I have already given the reason when comparing the tactics of Allenby with those of Titus. Allenby's campaign was the greatest and most successful of all the Palestine campaigns on record : greatest in the numbers engaged, greatest in the end attained. From the military point of view, Allenby's scheme was masterly. The Turkish line stretched from Gaza to Beersheba, and Allenby, combining sea and land power, resolved to drive the Turks from the former by capturing the latter. Beersheba fell on October 31, 1917, and Gaza a week after. Then came the advance on Jerusalem. It is quite clear that Allenby's plan must have been affected by the Maccabean precedent. The Syrians attempted to reach Jerusalem by the Beth-horon passes and failed ; by the Hebron road, and failed again. Allenby moved on both roads together, and succeeded.

First he advanced into Judea by the old road from Ramleh, through the Beth-horons, and by November 21 attained the ridge of Nebi Samwil, north-west of Jerusalem. He had done more than the Seleucids or Crusaders ever achieved, for as he himself wrote in his dispatch of December 16, 1917: 'The narrow passes from the plain to the plateau of the Judean range have seldom been forced, and have been fatal to many invading armies.' To Allenby they were not fatal. Allenby forced these passes and held them, while a wide sweep north-eastwards was made in a converging move-ment from Beersheba by the Hebron road on Jerusalem. Thus Jerusalem was isolated with a completeness which none but Titus had previously attained. But herein Allenby differed from Titus. I have already pointed out that we may justly be proud of the strategy of the British commander which compelled the Turks to evacuate their defences of the sacred sites without a blow. He manœuvred them out without a fight. Reims was bombarded, Jerusalem was not. It has been computed (I know not by what arithmetic) that that fall of Jerusalem was the twenty-third fall of the city. Let us hope that it will be the last. Bloodless as it was, let it be a good omen for an undisturbed peace.

To describe Allenby as a Crusader is inept. The latest Palestine campaign was fought, on both sides, by representatives of all the three creeds to whom Jerusalem is sacred. Of the Christian and Moslem troops engaged on our side I need say nothing. Their glory is known and will endure. But of the Jews engaged, a word may not be superfluous. Apart from the 'Judean' battalions, the 38th and 39th Royal Fusiliers, there was the 40th battalion, recruited entirely in Palestine on the basis of the older Zion Mule Corps. But besides these, there were many Jews among the Australian and New Zealander detachments, whose services were so conspicuous an element in Allenby's triumph.

It was assuredly fitting that Jerusalem should have fallen, peaceably, though after a fierce campaign, to representatives of Church, Synagogue, and Mosque—a symbol of that united love for the Holy Land on which its future prosperity and significance depend.

It is now the function of the spade to operate where once the sword raged: the spade of the farmer to recover the old fertility, the spade of the archaeologist to uncover the old sites. Palestine is to be recolonized, and its mounds excavated. The City of David is to be opened up. 'Not even the site of Troy, nor that of the Mycenae of Agamemnon, on both of which romance has been startlingly converted into realism, can compete in wealth of familiar association with the Judean acres which are now to be investigated.' And so the golden corn will rise in the valleys, and the secrets of history be revealed on the hills. And Palestine, the age-long battle-ground of races, dynasties, and creeds, shall be a battle-ground no more!

KEY TO PLATE

1. Head of Alexander with ram's horns. Silver tetradrachm of Lysimachus.
2. Head of Seleucus I in horned helmet. Silver tetradrachm.
3. Head of horned horse. Silver tetradrachm of Antiochus I.
4. Athena in quadriga of horned elephants. Silver tetradrachm of Seleucus I.
5. Apollo on omphalos. Symbol: head of horned horse. Silver tetradrachm of Antiochus IV. *Paris Cabinet*.
6. Zeus. Silver tetradrachm of Antiochus IV.
7. Nike driving four-horse car. Silver tetradrachm of Agrigentum.
8. Iudaea capta. Sestertius of Vespasian.
9. Iudaea devicta. Denarius of Vespasian.

Note.—All the above coins, except No. 5, are in the British Museum.

INDEX

Abbasid, 45.

'Abomination of Desolation', 20.

Acre, 46, 47; siege of, 43, 47; and Napoleon, 46–7; and Ibrahim, 47.

Acts, 6.

Aelia Capitolina, 38; founded, 40.

Aijalon, 25.

Aḳiba and Bar Cochba, 38 *n.*; travels in *Diaspora*, 38.

Alexander of Macedon, 5, 6, 44; and Antiochus IV, contrasted, 15; and Eastern cults, 8; and foreign shrines, 7; visit to Jerusalem, 7; A. and High Priest, 10; and Jaddua, 9, 11; policy towards Jews, 9–10, 12–13; and Judas compared, 23; and Napoleon compared, 8; and Omar compared, 8; and Paul's journeys, 6; siege of Gaza, 7; A. and Tyre, 7; A.'s character, 8; as a visionary, 10 sq.; 'two horned', 21 sq.; march to Pelusium, 11; night attacks, 21; use of phalanx, 24.

Alexandria, 47.

Alexandrian synagogue inscription, 12.

Ali Baba, 5.

Allenby, General, 1, 5, 43; his Palestinian campaign, 1, 4, 43, 47 sqq.; tactics, 47; use of Beth-horon and of Hebron roads, 30; advance on Jerusalem, 47; his army and malaria, 43; compared with Titus, 35, 36, 47 sq.; his conquest of Jerusalem, 48; Maccabaean precedents, 47.

American Civil War, 24.

Ammon and ram's horn, 21.

Amr, conquest of Egypt, 40 sq.

Anabasis of Alexander, 6.

Angora, 45.

Antioch, 17, 30.

Antiochus III, 13, 14; use of elephants, 30.

Antiochus IV, 14 sqq., 17 sqq., 26 sq.; attacks on Jerusalem, 18 sq.; campaigns in Egypt, 18; and Persia, 26; A. and *Daniel*, 18; death of, 26; use of elephants, 30; as a general, 26; and the Jews, 14 sq.; and *Maccabees II*, 18; his megalomania, 18; A. contrasted with Alexander, 15; compared with Ptolemy Philopator, 14 sq.; and with William II, 17; verdict of Tacitus, 26; and of Apocalyptic writers, 17; A. and Zoroastrianism, 26.

Antonia, 36.

Apis, 7.

Apocalyptic writers and Antiochus IV, 17.

Arabi Pasha, 47.

Arbela, 6.

Archer, T. A., cited on Crusades, 42.

Aristobulus taken to Rome, 32.

Aristotle and Maimonides, 14.

Armaments, systems of, compared, 25.

Arrian, 6; on Alexander's belief in omens, 11; on A.'s visit to Jerusalem, 11; on night attacks, 23; on use of phalanx, 25.

Arsuf, 44.

Artemis, Temple of, 26.

Ascalon, 12.

Assyrians, 5.

Athens and Jerusalem in epigram, 6.

Attacks on Jerusalem, direction of, 11 sq.

Autonomy, Jewish, and Rome, 32.

Azotus, 29.

Ba'al, 7.

Bacchides meets Judas, 31.

Bagoses, 9.

Bar Cochba, 35; alleged coincidences with other wars, 38 sq.; legends of, 39; in Ireland (!), 39; not of Davidic descent, 38 *n.*

Bar Cochba War, 37 sqq.; Büchler's view of, 38; local only, 38; *Seder 'Olam*, 39; victims, 39.

Beersheba, 12, 30, 47.

Beisan, siege of, 41.

Beit Nuba, 12.

Bethar, 38 *n.*

Beth-horon, 25, 47; road, 30.

Beth Zacharias, 30.

Bethzur, 29; fortified, 31.

Bernard of Clairvaux, 43.

Bevan, Edwyn, on Hellenism, 20.

Boer War and campaigns of Judas, 23 sq.

Bowmen, 25.

Breasted cited, 5.